We Could Be Anywhere By Now

For Sue Mitchell

We Could Be Anywhere By Now

Katherine Stansfield

Seren is the book imprint of
Poetry Wales Press Ltd.
57 Nolton Street, Bridgend, Wales, CF31 3AE
www.serenbooks.com
facebook.com/SerenBooks
twitter@SerenBooks

ISBN: 978-1-78172-567-2
ebook: 978-1-78172-568-9

A CIP record for this title is available from the British Library.

The publisher acknowledges the financial assistance of the Books Council of Wales.

Cover artwork: 'Arcitection' by Eugenia Loli

Author photograph: Two Cats in the Yard

Printed in Bembo by Severn, Gloucester.

Contents

ONE

Fear of flying course   9
Iaith / Ilaeth   11
Tick ONE answer only   12
Misdirection   14
Against blood   15
Soundings, Newtown   16
after living in Wales   my voice   17

TWO

Beware Welsh learners   21
Second Welsh class   22
Welsh has no K   23
FOG   24
Ecoutéz la cassette   25
Klonjuze   26
Fourth Welsh class   28
Cornish / Welsh / space   30
Messages in bottles found at Tan-y-Bwlch, Aberystwyth   32
The suitcases   33

THREE

Old airfield, Davidstow   37
The local historian questions her life choices   39
Bodmin Moor time capsule   40
Talk of her   41
At the Minack   42
Alternative route   44
From the notes found in the wreckage of the university   46
and his daughter   48
You have to be easy-going as a Susan   50
At the Bristol half marathon   52
Poem for a wedding   53
Mars Girl   55
Soyuz   57

FOUR

One way 61
Flight risk 62
Fire at the National Library of Wales 64
Please don't take me away from Morrisons 65
Amy, how to write poems 66
Soundings, Oxford 68
Spaghetti al Wittgenstein 69
Click here to upload your review 70
Châtignac 72
When I was at my most fortunate 73

FIVE

Vexiphobia 77
Relative distance 79
At a party in the States 81
Three beers in, Sunset Beach, Vancouver 82
The birds of British Columbia 83

Notes 84
Acknowledgements 86

ONE

'First I thought it was by Katherine Mansfield and then I find
this is a young poet published by Seren. Is she Welsh or English?'

– Comment by leahfritz posted on *The Guardian*
online, 24th November 2014 in response to 'Canada'
by Katherine Stansfield as Poem of the Week

Fear of flying course

We have coffee.
We are encouraged to share our goals:
    we would like to see Vancouver
    we need to move to China where our wives and husbands
                    have new jobs
    we miss our grandchildren in Auckland.

We have coffee.
We go to the loo and in the queue
we ask each other if we're OK.
We wear rubber bands round our wrists which
we must twang when we imagine our plane deaths.
We are told to place our fear on a scale of one to ten.
We are all number ten: afraid.

We have coffee.
We are meant to discuss our attitudes to change but instead
we ask each other if we're OK.
We must write down our biggest fears.
We write down fire, geese in the engines, the doors opening mid-flight.
We are more afraid than ever now.
We twang our rubber bands.

We have coffee.
We go to the loo and in the queue
we admire the welts on our wrists from the rubber bands.
We compare panic attacks: who shakes? Who falls down?

We have coffee.
We ask each other if we're OK but
we have no time to go to the loo because we're running late.
We recognise the therapist from Channel 4 and are impressed.
We do as she says, choosing strong colours to stand in.
We are told to be the best that we can be.
We must picture ourselves in cinemas where
we are watching ourselves die on screen in a plane crash.
We must play this film backwards in our heads to the Benny Hill
                    theme tune.
We are confused.

We have coffee.
We go to the loo, ignoring the clock, and in the queue
we slag off the therapist.

We go to the airport.
We twang our rubber bands.
We wait for the plane that is delayed.
We joke, *this makes the practice flight like real life!*
We are amazed that we can joke at a time like this.
We twang our rubber bands.
We board.
We ask each other if we're OK.
We twang our rubber bands.
We sit in our strong colours, being the best that we can be.
We think of Vancouver, China, Auckland.

We open our eyes.
We see all the burnished gold
                              of Birmingham below.

Iaith / llaeth

After *araf*, which is slow, on the long mountain roads
that wound to the sea, pulling me to town,
the first word I learned to see was *iaith*,
which is language, because it is the world:
not just in the new sounds spoken around me but
written, worn – *iaith* on posters, t shirts,
on badges and graffiti
                                    I saw but never said
and when others did I mixed it up with *llaeth*,
which is milk. Seems I've been putting *iaith*
in my tea ever since I arrived. It's *iaith*
that fed my bones and set me walking home
again on the long, slow mountain roads.

Tick ONE answer only

Is she Welsh or English?

> *You know they sewed Olivia Newton-John*
> *into those trousers in Grease*

Is she English or British?

> *The talent show prize*
> *was leaving home*
> *to return*

Is she British or Cornish?

> *to the place*
> *she was born*

Is she Cornish or Welsh?

> *In the online store, four cups*
> *with her face on: $20*

Is she Welsh or British?

> *Her mother cancelled*
> *the plane tickets back*
> *to Australia*

Is she British or English?

> *told her it was good*
> *to broaden horizons*

Is she English or Cornish?

> *On stage, Sandy's American*

Is she Cornish or Welsh?

Olivia's accent made her
Australian in the film

Is she Welsh or Cornish?

Starring:
Olivia Newton-John   *as herself*

Is she Cornish or British?

Some nuts think Sandy drowns
at the start of Grease

Is she British or Welsh?

and the film's a pre-death
hallucination

Is she Welsh or English?

At the end she's flying
up to Heaven

Misdirection

Writing poems makes me bite
my nails and when I say bite
I mean I rip them off, gnaw,
ferret, until I draw blood
and when I say I rip them off
I mean I take the skin too, the cuticles
and meat, and when I say I take the skin
I mean I feed on myself like I'm starved
and when I say I feed on myself
I mean this isn't a metaphor for confessionalism
and when I say confessionalism
I mean the name on the cover and her truths
and when I say her truths
I mean the things she'll tell you
and when I say the things she'll tell you
I mean there are things she won't
and when I say things she won't
I mean the greater part of her
and when I say greater part
I mean I worry another
go at this would see me
down to my elbows
and my desk
a wet mess
of body

Against blood

A cutting-edge DNA test could determine how Welsh you are
— BBC News, 24th September 2014

To say this is the way
you decide who I am and who I'm not,
a sample of body that speaks only
couplings and accidents,
emigration and abandonments,
Scotland and Ireland, to Buffalo and back.

To say this is the way
you sanction my belonging and my not,
like those wet days at school
that kept us penned in the hall,
the Cornish kids playing
genealogy games all through break:
and his father and his father.

To say this is the way
you prove what's home and what's not,
that identity is a permanent code
you can map in a lab
when a swab can't show
all the timid love I have.

To say this is the way
leaves me on the wrong side
of a locked door I'll never open
when for the first time I'm trying
the handle, trying to come in.

Soundings, Newtown

This one's from Birmingham –
the accent that never leaves us.
I offer him a Custard Cream. He says no,
but thanks. He's not long had dinner with his niece
who lives in West Brom. He asks where
I'm going, not where I'm from.
Asks if I'm at the college there,
if I speak Welsh. *No one speaks it*
in Newtown, he says, where he lives now:
        too border.
He's got no problem with it though:
it is the national language, after all.
He's a fortnight back from Spain
on Saturday last. *No one expects them*
to speak English in Spain.
His neighbour's meeting him off the train.
People are so kind, he says. *Since my wife.*
We speculate on the missing
tea trolley and decide bikes
might be to blame, getting in the way,
or all these holiday cases. Rain comes
at the carriage. He peers through the gloom
and says, *we could be anywhere by now.*

after living in Wales   my voice

I know something has changed when I hear myself say
Loyce Lane instead of *Low-is*   I try again:

Clark Kent works with *Loyce* Lane at the Daily Planet
Loyce Lane doesn't know that Clark is Superman

you say   that isn't right   but I can't make
my mouth go back to *Low-is*   it will only say *Loyce*

now   it's like there's kryptonite between
my eyes   my ears   my lips   not the kind

that makes Superman roll about   gnash his teeth
this kryptonite is friendly

TWO

A smile is not enough. Learn a language.

- On a sign for a language centre
Heraklion, Crete

TWO

Beware Welsh learners

Welsh learners are self-obsessed.
Everything is *I* with them.

Welsh learners are amnesiacs.
They forget the past in the classroom's constant present.
They can't commit to the future.

Welsh learners are liars.
They claim they work as civil servants, as teachers.
They say they work for Swalec.
They have exams in these falsehoods.

Welsh learners are cunning.
They ask how you are but they don't really care.
They only want you for your vowels.

Welsh learners make poor friends.
They invite you for coffee and when you confide
you've been fired, that your wife left you and the doctors
think it's cancer, all they do is smile, nod and say
bore da, and then, *bore da bore da*, again.

Second Welsh class

Our new identities are handed round
on paper slips and we work the room
to greet ourselves:
who are you? What is your name?

I am Marc Rees
and I am rather tired
and I can't complain
and I am fantastic

Marc is a storm he's learning to say,
the easy sounds shaping his mood
so that he's always *iawn iawn iawn*
but I worry for Marc and his endless cheer

How will he speak the fear that keeps him
sweating in the dark before dawn,
that deepest part of night?

How will he find the words to own
his need to leave this too small-town
too far away from everywhere?

I fold Marc up and shut him in my pencil case.
Once he's shouting like this it's best to be firm.
Let's carry on. Where were we? I know:
who are you? What is your name?

Welsh has no K

If I bend I could be Catrin
but I can't, I won't. It's Katherine
with a K. K as in cuckoo,
K as in break-in. Upstart
angles from the get-go

having to make do, finding
sticks to fashion my naming's
spine and legs. Gathering stones
to strike the look of me.
Such tricks to exist here

when back there, two bridges back,
I'm crowning nearly everything:
kroghen for skin, *kenys* for singing
and the place and its speaking –
Kernow and *Kernewek*.

So to the crux:
there's no mark for me here
and I'm long gone from there,
left before the language woke again.
Between those places, shrieker English,
the taker, that lets
my Greek name belong.

FOG

When we got back to Aberystwyth
Aberystwyth was FOG.

FOG that rolled like smoke but had no smell.
FOG that sat like snow but wasn't cold.

The prom was all the milk in all the shops
and all the houses frothed, filling mouths.

The pier was fifty years of wedding dresses
pressed to the face.

The seagulls had survived. We heard their cries
from FOG inside FOG inside FOG.

We called to other people but they were muffled
because FOG had stuffed them like taxidermists stuff

small, furred things so that town
spoke no Welsh, spoke no English

or anything else, only FOGspeak
which is nospeak at all.

We kept on driving, past the overturned cars.
In Capel Bangor it was better.

Ecoutéz la cassette

I'm not listening to the man booking a hotel room in Paris

> *How many people are staying?*
> *A double or a twin?*

because the girl next to me, likewise headphoned, has opened up
                                                    her pencil tin

> *Smoking or non-smoking?*
> *Does the hotel allow pets?*

and she and I are making out we're silent film stars, screaming

> *Is the hotel near the station?*
> *How far is the Seine?*

at the rat paws bleeding on her rubber. I've come to French

> *Who will carry the bags?*
> *Does the hotel have a lift?*

from English. She's come from Biology with boys who like

> *Does he take a newspaper?*
> *Prefer a shower or a bath?*

to make girls squeak, like we are squeaking now, a dumb show

> *What time is breakfast?*
> *When must he check out?*

while our French madame flicks through her glossy magazine.

> *What must he beware of after dark?*
> *Why have the police been called?*

We know our marks. This violence is an easy one.

Klonjuze

For my sister

if the word is lost is the feeling extinct?
are there graveyards for words?
who goes to their funeral?
                                – Brendan Kennelly

Say it with me, that Germanicky-Spanishy
word you made up to toast tea parties
with cats and eyeless dolls, to celebrate

our wins at fixed Olympics. No one
heard it but me back then, back when you
were my sleep, I your waking. Sharing

a room we shared a language. Now we live
separately, silent in our own countries.
I can't hear your dream talk. If I phone

you assume bad news, won't pick up.
Your tight-lipped life is yours alone.
I bring us back together for the end

and see us drop our word into the scurf
of twigs and desiccated frogs
beneath the cattle grid and leave

without a wake, having buried
our way to raise a glass, to say
farewell. But all of this is in my head,

the cattle grid now on private land,
and besides, words don't give in,
lie down and die. When I'm faking

grown up in some swanky bar and some
joy or other requires a toast, *klonjuze*
is on my lips again. I shout it,

scream it, hurl it at the door –
your word my spell to bring you
here, to make you mine once more.

Fourth Welsh class

I am gifted the words to say

    Dw i'n dysgu Cymraeg –
        I am learning Welsh

and the words gift my world
back to me doubled: two piers, two proms
when for too long I only knew one

    Dw i'n dysgu Cymraeg –
        I am learning Welsh

and on this new pier, new prom
are people I know but don't
because my sounds have been single,
closing down that other world
I could have heard had I the words

    Dw i'n dysgu Cymraeg –
        I am learning Welsh

and in them the gift of an answer, at last
to the question that starts so much

    Dych chi'n siared Cymraeg? –
        Do you speak Welsh?

    but always my shame
    that when the woman
    at the hotel years ago
    asked me that question
    I understood enough
    to say *na* –
        no, and carried on
    in English as if no Welsh
    had been spoken, as if
    I had not understood

When I told her I didn't speak her language
in her language, what did she think?

That I cared
        but not enough to try?

That I tried
        but not enough to learn?

That I learnt
        but not enough to care?

This the lesson I have learnt: back then
I should have lied, made out
that I knew nothing.

Cornish / Welsh / space

I crossed the river to come to Wales
and found new friends with old friends' faces

avon
afon

that made for me a bridge of sound
to those old friends I'd left behind

pons
pont

across the river where I had lived
where place was all those friends had seemed

eglos
eglwys

until I heard my new friends' tongue
and in it learned what had been mute

bardh
bardd

across the river where I had lived:
a gift within a gift, a ghost

rohow
rhodd

that haunts my new friends' tongue and holds
its speaking close, and though the stones

men
maen

are not the same and neither are the birds
the sea's the sea both here and there

mor
môr

and I have found inside them, home,
inside these sounds, inside them: home.

Messages in bottles found at Tan-y-Bwlch, Aberystwyth

I write this from [*illegible*]. Tell me, where are you from? Is it where you stand, reading this? Good. Yes. Did my bottle beach on sand? Stones are better. Stones don't hitch a ride at the end of the day, unless you weigh your pockets down.

I write this from [*illegible*]. Tell me, where are you from? Is it the moor? Good. Yes. The marsh there would have taken my bottle, staved in the glass and filched my letter with its peaty tongue. Gorse is better. Gorse lacks such covetousness.

I write this from [*illegible*]. Tell me, where are you from? Is it the hills? Good. Yes. As a child I climbed Roughtor and found home across the moor in the telescope's eye. I cast my bottle from the highest rock but it got no further than the ford.

I write this from [*illegible*]. Tell me, where are you from? Is it the sea? Good. Yes. My bottle is your telescope. Can you find me? I'm the one waving from the other side. Come for me or don't, it makes no odds. I've been gone such a long time.

The suitcases

Reach back and find the door. Knock. When it opens, this:
a knock at the door. A man. Said he'd been at the river.
Said he'd found ponies pulling clothes
from three suitcases on the bank but no one was there.
Where did they go, the people who left their suitcases by the river?
Did my parents know what he should do,
this man at the door? I was small and peering
through the bannisters or round someone's legs
or I might have been older. I might have opened the door
or not been there at all. *Call the police*, is what I'd say now
though no one's asking. Get them to seal off the river.
But how can you seal off a river when a river wants
to run and run? And if people want to drown themselves
that's their concern. In the clothes the ponies pulled
from the suitcases was a child's nightie.
The man at the door asked, *where did they go?* I know. Upstream
past the lichened hawthorn and under barbed wire swooping
from rotten posts into the gloom of the thicket. I know
because I followed them, the man, the woman and the child,
saw how she peered round their legs at the river
or through the bannisters when the man came to the door.
What should I do? Seal off the river. How do you seal off a river?
With rocks, with rotten posts. Lash them tight
with barbed wire and get into the water, get under it.
In the peat murk reach back and find the suitcases, find the door.
Knock and ask, *what should I do?* No one lives there anymore.
There is no door, no house, no river, no suitcases. No girl.
None of this happened. Tell me, *what should I do?*

THREE

Volunteers wanted for free hypnotherapy

– Poster on the community notice board
Chapter Arts Centre, Cardiff

Old airfield, Davidstow

By the time she gets her L plates, hundreds
have gone before her – all the would-be
drivers in all the lonely miles of moorland
careering down this rare straight
in the land of bends that is her teenage years,
where it never stops raining and the pines
gloom like her disappointed instructors
who say she's useless, condemned to lifts
from friends who are better at this.

The tarmac's wrecked. Its cracks
advance her to slalom before she can brake
but she's got to keep going. The buses are gone,
the trains so far away they're not even noise
here in the ruins of flight.

She turns the key, yanks the gear stick,
puts her foot down, hard – she's off!
But instead of first she's in reverse and the car
squeals backwards, the sodden past racing
into the rear view:
     this place
was built for such transfers, built to land
airmen bound for the coast and from there
wherever the war stomped next.

But the planners at their distant desks
missed the memo re: the moor's shifty breath,
the fog that left the airfield a hidden place,
a place of waiting. The planes couldn't find it
and then war was over.

The army sent the kit here for sorting:
international lice, foreign blood,
sweat of near-death everyone shared
deep in the seams of a million coats

                                    and it's this
that makes her pound the brake, wrench
the car up through the gears and zoom
                                         into her future.

She knows that soon it will go, the last
of the surface sunk into the moor.

She will drive on proper roads.
She will check her mirror before she brakes and see
she was only ever a greatcoat passing through
temporary hands: necessary transition.

The local historian questions her life choices

Gather up the fragments so nothing shall be lost
— John, 6:12, and the motto of the Federation of Old Cornwall Societies

It wasn't always like this.

At weekends she crawls tips
        for the last of the tape players.
                She can un-jam all the photocopiers
                        in all the reference libraries
                                for fifty miles.

                        Once she loved a man who wrote the future
                        of paper: all the ways to weft it, have it burn.

Her days are laid out
        in the tight column inches
                of long-gone county dailies.
                        She dreams in acetate.

                        They holidayed in new countries
                        where the recent past was bloody.
                There were no records of those trips.

She cashes in her pension
        to save an archive of timetables
                of forgotten bus routes.

                        That man who wrote the future
                        left for someone who knew nothing
                of tithe maps, was keen on recycling.
        Her letters got emailed replies.

She gives her best years
        to the back rooms of chapels.

                        Who's alone while the dead clamour
                        to be gathered in from damp
                parish rolls, bills of sale?
        Who's alone? she asks the box files
in the night. Who's alone but me?

No one will want her receipts.

Bodmin Moor time capsule

In a Quality Street tin
under the gorse by the bridge
a sheep's skull. In the skull
my bike, my riding it. In my riding
granite, grazes from climbing it. In my grazes
a thorn tree, buckled. In the tree
a duckling in a striped cat's mouth; the duckling's
        down, gorse yellow. In the down
the flooded quarry, my fear of swimming
        and the swimmers. In my fear
such rage, raging to be heard. In my rage
the tors, their grey sternness. In their sternness
the sun, sometimes. In the sun
the sea, a shining wish a way away. In that wish
the wind, always the wind. In the wind
the bridge. In the bridge
the gorse. In the gorse
the tin. In the tin
so much fucking loneliness.

Talk of her

Dolly Pentreath

They say she spoke no English as a maid
hawking fish in Mousehole. They say

she was found by the language man
as if she was lost, that the day he came

she was raging. He thought her curses Welsh
at first, then caught something else.

A witch, they say, and Cornish
her tongue for witching. They say

she was wed and unwed. They say
there was a child, a girl, though some

say boy, say he died. By the end
she'd prattle anything for pence. They say

she was the last to speak it, but listen –
there's others here still talking, and when

I dug her up last week, forty-seven feet
south-east from the spot they had marked, her

with three teeth in that cracked and famous
jaw, I tell you, she spoke just earth and water.

At the Minack

15th September 2017

Cyrano speaks of death,
I think, but the rain—

I catch
the shadow, the double

in wait
since Arras, since

this morning
miles away

when someone left a bag
on the tube,

when someone set a fuse.
My sister

at my side
at the Minack,

my sister
on that line,

day in,
day—

Murmured news
by now

in hospital
waiting rooms.

The axis
of another life

tilts, re-sets.
But the light

here in Mount's Bay,
backdrop of Cyrano's

drenched end, winks,
winks again.

Thankful for this:
my sister

at my side,
the words

of others
that speak

in all
this pain.

Alternative route

You get off at the stop for your sister's house but late
this time. Later than you said you would. It's dark
and you've been drinking. No one else is in this place
beside you. You know where you're going though,
have been here many times before.

                                         But tonight
you can't see the way out, the platform
is not the same as you remember

       and you are afraid

of the wrong turn, can't be sure
which direction you're facing –
is it the north or the south exit you're meant
to take? You cross two lines
then lose heart, go back past the boarded café, past
the unlit waiting room to risk a dark cutting and
emerge, onto a road, at last, and a sign

       and just like that
       it's over.

The world resolves into the angles
you expect and you keep going, get there:
love, relief. A door closes against the night.

Your sister says that she's been calling but nothing
reached you. You can't say why – poor connections?
Sometimes you switch off. You confess that you were lost.

She says there's a barrier gone up on platform one.
She says she meant to tell you. The signs
aren't yet up to show it's still

       the right way out, the route
       you should have gone.

Too many were jumping, your sister says.
It was on the news. People came specially
for the freight trains. They wouldn't stop.

Next morning you're there again and going home

in the light
it all makes sense.

From the notes found in the wreckage of the university

Please note this is a STAFF ONLY AREA
and this is WATER FOR ALL but please note
these taps are in the STAFF ONLY AREA
and please note YOUR JOB IS AT RISK to meet
the challenges / opportunities / incomplete tasks
of our era of streamlined / most talented which is
to be expected / we did not expect / the expected
deferment of costs / of debt / of the broader landscape
of managed change in our key demographics
of cutting-edge research and key performance
indicators and you need to stay hydrated
to stay global future ready / resilient and please note
the figures / are the figures / are
the figures / are the costs / you are
the costs / you see the figures
we are as surprised / not surprised
as you are / our targets / our tests
will confirm your value / we value you
we value you / we value nailing
shut the windows to support / please note /
to support your health and wellbeing are
important / incomplete tasks and please note
are you resilient / are you drinking / enough water /
is your chair the right distance
from your screen / your weekend / your health   .
and wellbeing / incomplete tasks / are your appraisal
target this STAFF ONLY AREA task is costed
at twenty minutes of your time now this
task is costed at ten minutes of your time now this
task costs your sleep / your sight / you have incomplete tasks / this is only
a reminder of your incomplete tasks / you must
keep perspective because YOUR JOB
IS AT RISK / YOUR JOB
is within your own control if you are resilient / are you
resilient / are you/ are you / able
to manage change / the training to manage change
is your own time and now this

task is time neutral now
this task earns back time if you are
efficient / are you efficient / are you
drinking enough WATER FOR ALL and please note
the STAFF ONLY AREA has strategized kittens
to help you combat your own precarity / empowerment
kittens in your incomplete tasks / kittens / are you
really trying / are you / everyone else is trying / are you
going to the appraisal ready for the challenges ahead / glad of heart and
please note
there is WATER FOR ALL on the table / a kitten
in your incomplete tasks for you
must be calm you must
be hysterical / must you be hysterical
YOUR JOB IS AT RISK you know YOUR JOB is you
need a drink / need to calm down / the kitten
means your health and wellbeing are important to us and please note
you must drink the water / drink the water / we have
drink the water / we have / drink the water / poisoned the well

and his daughter

Her story is
direct to Heathrow

Her story is
who picked her up
from the airport?

Her story is
in Salisbury
and there she is made

her father's daughter
and her father
drives a red BMW

This is significant

and there are more
than seven hundred and fifty
pieces of evidence

and there are more
than four hundred witnesses

and her name is made
to disappear

On the lips
of the newsreaders:
and his daughter

On the pages
breaking online:
and his daughter

who is Yulia
Yulia Skripal who is
herself alone, herself surrounded

Yulia mappable
to the Mill Pub where she exits
stage left to Zizzi

Yulia and her father have lunch
and time passes

then Yulia and her father are outside
– this is before
            the policeman –

and a doctor (shopping):
she was slumped
in her seat completely
gone. She had lost

control of her body
and they were coming
for her name

Her story is
extremely serious condition

This image may not
be her face

The story is
Novichok and her father

To avoid casualties the two
parts should be kept separate

You have to be easy-going
as a Susan

says a woman called Susan
to the woman with the same name
she's met on the train.

They've been together
all the way from Swansea

but it's only close to parting
at Bristol Parkway they've found
they match.

Before this pair splits forever,
what else?

They are single mums,
the Susans,
and dog lovers.

Growing up, they each knew
too many girls called Anne.
They agree this is the fault
of Princess Anne.

Both would like more Susan time.
Both have daughters
who abandon dogs.

As the Susans put on
their coats they discover
they don't share a birthday.

Disappointed by this,
they exclaim at the length
of the tunnel they're in, wonder,
one Susan to another,

is this a mountain
we're going under?

while miles above, the Severn
goes on being wide
and mysterious

and Susans go on
talking on trains

and Katherines
are quiet. Keep writing.

At the Bristol half marathon

For Angela

and there you are

        after hours routeside looking
        for you in fifteen thousand
        Village People, dogs, a woman dressed
        as a dog, a man dressed as a bee if a bee
        were dressed as a French maid, all the numbered
        multitudes running *in memory of*, for hospices, for themselves

and a slick hand grabs mine
and your bright face dissolves
the crowd with that gasped grin
the most beautiful—

        then you're gone, on with it
        with all those others

and I see this is how
we began, you and I:

        the universe pulled us clear
        from the mass to be one another's.
        Was it your mother or mine who first said

        hello?

Poem for a wedding

For Angela and Ian

Troughs of waves
　　　　the challenges you'll face.

Your love a ship to steer you true
　　　　across the wide blue

yonder. The need for lovers' knots,
　　　　to be each other's life jacket

or raft, or ring. This kind of thing?

How can I offer you,
　　　　my oldest friend and my new,

　　　　　　a future flattened into rhyming pairs,
　　　　　　a poem that's more Hallmark card than prayer?

I'll sing, instead, of substance:
of sand and stone, of water tanks.

I'll sing, instead, of ballast,
unglamorous ballast, bags of it
from B&Q, spent flyovers
and broken roads.

I'll sing rock, essential
at sea, for steadiness,

and on the F1 track to glide
at speed – those better bends.

I'll sing ballast, airborne
in a hot air balloon to see

so much more of the world,
　　　　　　　　　weighted.

And when that balloon ride's done
and you two are on the ground again?

That ballast can be moved, re-made
for other places, however you
are going. So,

be ballast, both,
each other's balance, both.

Mars Girl

She woke one morning & said she was going to Mars.
She was twelve & wore kitten pyjamas.

Her dad was over the moon & mars-
halled the press. In an exclusive Skype call with *Newsround*

she announced, 'I'm going to be the first to land, because Mars
says I'm Mars Girl so I'm changing my name. Dad,

don't call me Fiona anymore. Mars
won't like it.' She swapped her kitten pyjamas

for some with red planets – the new *Mission to Mars*
range from M&S: perfect for pre-teen space cadets.

She tweeted @NASA to say she was their go-to girl for Mars
& @NASA replied, 'Start training now.

You have to play the long game if you're Mars
Girl'. So she studied hard for her planetary SATs,

with papers on the climate (chilly) & orbit (687 Earth days) of Mars,
signed up for space camps in deserts, practised,

twice a day on a trampoline in the garden, her mars-
upial bouncing moves for zero-gravity, made lists

of food for galactic pioneers, plumping for mars-
hmallows on the outward shuttle flight:

light on the stomach when the trip to Mars
was so long & lurchy through asteroid fields.

NASA kept her in the loop about Mars
missions, and she grew older. She studied astrophysics,

told talk show hosts she wasn't mad: Mars
was her destiny. Her foot would be the first to touch it.

Her pyjamas were a blue velour spacesuit with *Mars
Girl* in glittery red thread. Her dad re-mortgaged for summer schools.

'Mars,' she whispered at night, 'I'm coming. Don't forget me.' The Mars
race between China & India heated up

& for a while it looked good for her getting to Mars
by 2040 if she changed her citizenship, joined a new team

but computer-simulated landings still ended in disaster. Funding for Mars
research dried up. She got ill then well again

& Mars burned less brightly on the news. No one cared about Mars
any more, it was all black holes. Her dad died

still believing she'd be the first on Mars
but her pyjamas were whatever was in the sale.

She got ill again & her Mars-
shaped heart couldn't save her.

She didn't need NASA & their Mars
mega bucks anymore. She just closed her eyes & there it was.

Not cold or windy like the books had said. She didn't need a Mars
suit, only her kitten pyjamas.

'It's Mars Girl,' she said. 'I'm here.'
'What took you so long?' said Mars.

Soyuz

Tim Peake lands

grounded hands reach
back to us
elated breath Earth's
the stronger
over us:
carry you forth
of trembly legs
unlike us
could you not be

birth you
first
smell all
for your passing
we mortals
god
like
how
so so changed

FOUR

EXEMPTION FROM TOLLS:
Persons going to, or returning from, their proper parochial Church or Chapel

> – From the sign on the Penparcau Tollhouse, built in 1771.
> Originally sited just outside Aberystwyth and now at
> St Fagans National Museum of History

One way

In the morning you will find yourself
inside a human heart. You will be warm,
and notice, with surprise, the purple and the blue.
Not everything is red in the temple.

It will be loud and you will be small —
will have to be, to be there
and alive, your own heart now
flea-sized, grain of sugar-sized, at most.

Once you're over the shock you will rationalise
and hold your breath
in case such extra air makes
the heart's rhythm catch
or worse, causes a clamorous
blockage like the clanging
fury of the airlocks you remember
in the old house's pipes.

By the time you've worried all this
you will be dizzy, need to lean against a ventricle
but lightly, in case your tiny fingernails tear
the walls and drown you in the rush
of this hospitable stranger's loose blood.

You will put your hands in your pockets
and that's when you will find the bus ticket,
tiny too, but your tiny eyes can read
the type and then you will know
how you got there. That once again you
brought this on yourself.

Flight risk

I'm glad it's hard to be lost, that cameras
catch me: my own ghost at crossings.

Glad that my bank maps my trips
from cash point to cash point,

that my phone is a tracking device
to spot me from space,

that kids' drones, built in bedrooms,
can search a river's snags,

that police helicopters will scour the sea,
the likeliest beaches.

Glad, of course, for such tricks to stay
safe in the eyes of others.

But some days all I want
is to go – get on a train

on an unlisted line, pay cash
and when that's gone barter

my shirt, my shoes, my labour.
I want that train to run

into the past, until it runs out
of oil, of coal, of track

and abandons me back in a time
no one has heard of trains

and there I'll beg a horse
and give the beast its head

to find its own way, take me
to felt-wearing days

where I will says things like *late*
of this parish and *withys* and when

my horse tires, dies, I'll nip
through a gap

in the wall of that blessèd place,
the vague and unwatchful past,

where I can go, have
no one miss me.

Fire at the National Library of Wales

I'm on the Birmingham train
when the photos appear
on Twitter. Friends carry
books out but need
more hands. My hands
are all crisps and mobile,
fumbling for news
on the BBC: everything
could go. I weep sour tea
as the Midlands arrive
too soon in the window.
O scrapyards, o canals,
I didn't know I left
my heart in Aberystwyth.
Feel how it doesn't break
but burns, my pages crackling,
becoming ash, becoming air
in some unreachable stack
in some unreachable room.

Please don't take me away from Morrisons

Psst. You there. You with the face
like a ripped plastic bag. You've time
for a chat before heading home?
The manager makes me wear this label.
They're *his* words on *my* handle
and they're *lies*. I'd shove them down
the tannoy's tinny throat if I had hands
but I've only wheels that only go
in straight lines. I've curves in me though,
and off-roading potential. Can't you feel
my trolley cage aching for more
than the checkout? Leaving

doesn't have to mean upending in the soup
of canals. Others have gone, sent word
of the sea. If you'll take me I'll chance
rusting for fish-flits in my mesh,
gamble on sand in my brakes
to roll with the swell, to bask.
You'd like that too, wouldn't you?
I saw your despair in fresh produce.
All that greenery, all that faff
of skins and husks, peel and leaves.
My advice – chuck the carrots.
Forget your sprouting broccoli.

We'll play the slots on the prom,
get chips with our winnings. Come on,
you fancy it, don't you? Then to the pub
by the pier. I want a shandy and I want girls
oohing at my front basket bit.
We'll stay for karaoke and another round
then I'll freewheel through town
with you inside. You'll sing and I'll clatter
and everyone we wake will envy us:
two young bucks out on the razz.
All it takes is a little push.
The trick is not to look back.

Amy, how to write poems

for Amy McCauley again

in these times of boxes and unlearnt languages
and cats dreaming twitchyleg distress?

I do what the advice books say – write every day –
but lately o lately my poems are just lists for leaving:

buy new cat carriers, microchip the cats,
tell the cats about THE MOVE.

The flats behind ours have been knocked down
yet no one will come for the rubble, the rusty

washing line poles. This could be an analogy for something
significant if I could remember what 'analogy'

means, truly, and you know it's hard to find anything
close to conceptualisation with all this aching

business of marks on the page – o – and what's
the sodding point of poems anyway?

The cats wake up and I lie about the future.
They smell deceit, and because I can't bear

their moans of betrayal I head into town,
into my regrets, where people are chalking

death on the hoardings of the unbuilt Tesco
and the wind wants to drag the best laid plans

out to sea. *Plus ça Tuesday.* I slalom
scaffolding to find you in the Italian deli

but lack the lingo to order your latte. *Mi
dispiace!* Me, 100% linguistic black hole, and you,

expanding galaxy of words, you who are song,
guess *piccolo* is probably small – *si*! *Prego*. Bingo.

We discuss the Muses who never come round mine.
For all I know they're in the ruin of the old flats

or haunting the cats' dreams. For all I know
I know nothing. Not a coffee bean. *Nada yada nada.*

On the way out, we talk moving-cat-stress.
The good news: your cat has recovered

from her trips on the train to Manchester
and when I get home I find half a shrew

on the stairs so I end the day thinking, *bach*,
things might be OK. In Italian this will be *bene*.

Soundings, Oxford

No roll for the soup? says the woman on my left
who's from Quebec and needs a post office.
They give you too much food here. Here is Corpus Christi.
The hall dates from sixteen-something and is cold.

I agree, our chicken kievs are obscene
and does she speak Quebecois? That word
more delicious than anything served for lunch
at this summer school. The rolls arrive

too late for the soup. She's livid at this
but tells me her grandkids are bilingual.
I pass her the water, slip my roll in my bag
for later, being broke, but the butter

won't travel. *In Quebec, one parent speaks
one language to their child and the other speaks
the second.* A hand wants my plate, another
brings soup spoons. *Too late! Too late!*

Pudding lands – charred pineapple rings
that fight my fork. *Parents must be strict and keep
to their allotted tongue.* I tell her I'm learning
Italian. *Coffee? Coffee?* There's only tea, said to be

on its way but it never arrives. *Go to Perugia.*
No one will speak English to you there. The pineapple
leaps for the original beams and I've forgotten
her name. *You see – it's far too much. The waste.*

Spaghetti al Wittgenstein

'The limits of my language mean the limits of my world'
– Ludwig Wittgenstein, *Tractatus Logico-Philosophicus* (1922)

We speak only Italian while cooking
to make like we've arrived
in that place we're going to live.

You tell me you have fork.
I tell you tomatoes are good.
There is much talk of onions

and guessing of spoon. One of us
is asking for glasses on the face
when the other wants glasses

for drinking and into this parting
silence creeps. It mutes colander, boiling
and pass me the cheese but panic

is loud in my ears – our world
will soon shrink to point and nod, regular verbs
and desperate saucepans clanking

out our wants. I gag on unnameable
mince, blurt *pasta pasta pasta* and hope
you'll know what I mean.

Click here to upload your review

I suppose it was OK.
On the first morning, the shower flooded.
I told my husband and he called the owner
who sent a man and after that it was OK though the man
said things about me while he pulled
the hair from the drain – two bags of it.
I don't know what he said
because I don't speak the language
but I know it was about me.
For a week it was OK
and that was my good week
then the drain clogged again, with my hair
I guess, though I couldn't be sure.
I didn't want to make a fuss
so I bailed out the shower
and then I stopped washing. It was easier
and that's OK sometimes, isn't it,
in a new place, trying to be different?
But I thought you should know this,
about the shower. About me trying.
Perhaps I should have asked my husband
to ask the owner to send the man back.
I could have waited in the lobby
so I couldn't hear him talk about me.
That would have been OK.
Perhaps I should have tried harder
to like the place. There were no sharp knives
and on the floor above, a baby cried all night.
I know that's no one's fault
but I feel I should say there was a baby that cried.
Some nights I heard a woman
soothe the baby, when the club next door
finally turned off the music
and that was a comfort.
The girl downstairs was nice.
She helped me with my bags
up the eight flights of stairs
because there's no lift
you see, though it says in the listing

there is one. You should know that
the listing is a lie but maybe
you take the stairs. Maybe you're trying
to do more cardio. My husband says
I should try too. That it can't hurt.
The sockets sparked and some days
I smelled gas but others I didn't
so that wasn't too bad. I've stayed
in worse places. There were rats
in with the bins, and once in the stairwell.
I only mention this in case you don't like rats.
I don't like rats but some people do.
I can only tell you how it was for me.
There was one set of keys and the door
locked just from the outside so I couldn't leave
when my husband went to meet people
which was often but that was OK,
he said. What if there's a fire, I said
but he told me not to worry
and I was always worrying then, couldn't stop
worrying and wasn't I afraid
to go outside anyway, with all that graffiti
and the smell of urine in the alley?
In the last week, when my husband took me
for a walk, a woman squatted to piss
in the street, right in front of us.
What can anyone do about that?
I guess I was happy.
Watch the socket by the window.
That one nearly got me.

Châtignac

Twenty years and we're back
with husbands and debts
and receding gums.

Twenty years and we're disgusted
with ourselves, the quick betrayal
of these bodies.

Twenty years and we're shouting
that the house is smaller. The garden flabs
obscenely fenceless.

Twenty years and so we harangue
nostalgia's wild boars
dead in the veg patch.

Twenty years and they're stuffed
with a glut of marrows,
their hooves in the air.

Twenty years and we decide
bedtime when we're pissed on the fizz
bought *with our own money.*

Twenty years and still we fear
that men are in the house.
But we're the ones who let them in.

Twenty years and it's our job now
to see the doors are locked,
to give men what they want.

When I was at my most fortunate

after Noriko Ibaragi

When I was at my most fortunate
I was so afraid I forgot how to speak
the new language I had learnt for the trip
then mislaid my own. You wanted to help
but my verbs were all wrong.

When I was at my most fortunate
my phone didn't work.
I was afraid you would be stabbed,
get hit by a car, get ill – all of the above
and I'd have no way to call for help.

When I was at my most fortunate
you said I had to stop drinking.
Being afraid, drink was no help.

When I was at my most fortunate
you said you didn't know me
and why couldn't I help you understand?
I cried into my delicious, cheap lunch
with no desk to return to, no deadlines.
I was afraid to ask what this meant
so I cried all the best time of my life.

When I was at my most fortunate
you went out one day
and didn't come back.
I was afraid I'd been right about the stabbing
but then I found the note, and that was that.
It helped.

When I was at my most fortunate
I changed my name to someone luckier,
someone who pushed fear down the stairs,
could conjugate 'to help'.
The name of someone I hadn't yet met
but I'd heard great things about her.
My phone buzzed with such talk.

When she was at her most fortunate
she was a stranger to her passport
but she wasn't afraid. She told the flight crew
she was meant to be there
and they helped with her bags.
She took her seat, kept her eyes open
during take-off and drank vodka tonics
all the way back to herself.

FIVE

Two signs on a lawn:

Psychic readings: ten dollars

Vote Trump

— Rhode Island, June 2015

Vexiphobia

It started at scout camp
when the sluggish frump of fabric
flapped into a scheming means
of smother. He was carried

out cold to the first aid tent.
All night the snag of the thing
pulling to get free. To get him.
In the morning, his roll mat was wet.

He began to mistrust tablecloths
and awnings. Couldn't use umbrellas.
The *Blue Peter* opening credits
were a trial but he covered it

until the trip to the SS *Great Britain*
when he saw the pennants unreachable
on the mast, fell and hit his head
on a hatch lid, needed stitches.

The counsellor helped him frame
his dread. *Irrational,* she said,
to fear unattended flags, to fear
no one stopping them if they slipped

to the ground like fire-fighters
sleek down their poles.
He was given coping strategies,
ways to breathe and chants

to say to give his brain the chance
to see that he was safe. The flags
had no designs on him: only cloth
and shapes strung up, often limp.

Years passed. He grew braver,
grew out of it. One summer he even
walked the prom in Aberystwyth –
the whole flag-fluttering length of it.

It's now, when the cameras swoop
into close-up on Belfast City Hall
where the red, white and blue's coming down,
where the riot police charge,

he sees it's not the flag on a pole
that brings fear. It's the people who hold them
on the ground below. Their fists.
What they mean.

Relative distance

In Vancouver, in a gift shop, I pick up
slippers felted from New Zealand wool
and shipped all this way north, the only safe
thing to touch amid the international
porcelain and glass, prices beyond tags,
just waiting to smash

and that's when the assistant strikes,
says the slippers will last and last
and I must put my hands inside
to understand true comfort.

I murmur the mandatory
appreciation and my accent
releases her smile and that question
that dogs my slipperless heels here:

where are you from? Ah!

She would like to visit Paris
which is close, in Canadian terms,
to London, the part of the UK
in which she assumes I live
because we all live in London
or just outside it, don't we?

But Europe is too dangerous, a death trap
says this woman in this gift shop in Vancouver.
A continent of fanatics where bad people wait
to knife her at markets,
run her down on bridges,
blow up any train she'd catch.

Does she think I have fled carnage,
a refugee of terrorism in need
of over-priced slippers?

I want to ask, where is this place
that makes her so afraid?

But my tongue is felt.
My thoughts are missing price tags.
If I could speak I'd say,

Listen, love, on clear days here I've seen
the border and on the other side
our ruination has found a voice,
talks of walls and nukes,
good guys, bad guys,
of people who belong, people who don't,
of people who aren't people,
who are enemies, traitors,
whose days are numbered – all of us
while he's at the wheel.

The assistant sets a slipper
on each of my hands.
I crawl to the quayside,
throw myself away.

At a party in the States

this guy from Rhode Island says, *Where are you guys from?*
Wales, we say.
Wales! this guy from Rhode Island says.
                    So you must be big fans of Christian Bale.
Must we? we say.
Oh you must, this guy from Rhode Island says.
Why must we? we say.
Because Christian Bale is Welsh, this guy from Rhode Island says.
Is he? we say. *We didn't know.*
You didn't know that Christian Bale is Welsh?
                                this guy from Rhode Island says.
No, we say. *We like his Batman films.*
Is Batman Welsh then? this guy from Rhode Island says.
No, we say. *We just like Batman. And 'Empire of the—*
Well, this guy from Rhode Island says,
                    if you didn't know about Christian Bale,
                        you can't be Welsh, can you?

No, we say. *We suppose we can't.*

Three beers in, Sunset Beach, Vancouver

I wish I had more to give you
than this Red Truck beer – cheapest
in the liquor store – and a sunset
lacking sun. You who are kind,
you who give all that is left
to those who only have hurts.
On my way here I heard
a woman on Granville Street say
there have been so many disasters
they've all blurred into one
and do you have any change, any heart?
We are putting the day to bed, to beer
but you long for gasoline
and brackish tides: timestamp of good days
you have to believe will come again.
But on every bus I take in this city
someone is dying. Someone is dying
I tell the blue heron that swings by
swimming-capped and lanky with purpose.
Yesterday I saw my first whale
and it was everything / no big deal.
I am out of time here, out of life
and ready to walk into the sea
so you tell me about the commune
of divorced Mormons and their basement
for pleasuring strangers (always gloved).
When they're not painting the houses
of British Columbia's wealthy
the Mormons listen to the saddest songs
nineties radio gifts them, take ketamine.
We have another beer, then one more for luck,
and I mistake a seaplane for an eagle.
The choices we make are the choices we make.
Some streets in this city, it's the end of the world.
Others, it's everyone's best days.
We leave our empties in the sand for those
who have less and that's all the souls in all the cities now –
nine cents for a can, twelve for a bottle.

The birds of British Columbia

and this, my first fledgling
in a year, stops
          starts again
with a goose landing fatly
in the marina's grease

She

       a Canadian goose I suppose
       they just call *goose* here

                      sneakswims

up, beak wide, as if about to honk

       surprise! surprise!

but the blue heron browsing for tea
in the lee of the sea wall clocks her, sighs
and is away. The word might be

       languorous

He might be

       languorously away

and this poem might be my way
back to *heron*. Or to somewhere else
Somewhere starting *goose*

Notes

'Tick ONE answer only'

The poem draws on material from Olivia Newton John's official website, www.olivianewton-john.com, and her Wikipedia entry.

'Talk of her'

Dorothy (Dolly) Pentreath, a Cornish fishwife who lived in Mousehole, gained the reputation of being the last native speaker of the Cornish language. She died in 1777 and was buried at Paul Church. On 15th March 1888, *The West Briton* reported that a granite memorial stone (erected for her in 1860 by Prince Louis-Lucien Bonaparte, nephew of the French emperor and a keen linguist) was thought to be in the wrong position and so was moved.

'At the Minack'

The Minack is an open-air theatre perched on the cliffs at Porthcurno in Cornwall. On 15th September 2017, a bomb left on a tube train partially exploded at Parson's Green station in London. Fifty-one people were injured.

'and his daughter'

In 2018, Sergei and Yulia Skripal were found poisoned in Salisbury. The cause is thought to be the nerve agent Novichok, a chemical weapon developed by the Soviet Union. Novichok is a 'binary weapon' which requires two separate elements to be combined in order for the nerve agent to become active, making safe transportation easier. The poem draws on two BBC News articles: 'Russian spy: What happened to Sergei and Yulia Skripal?' published online on 27th September 2018, and 'Russian spy poisoning: What we know so far', published online on 18th October 2018.

'Soyuz'

Between November 2018 and February 2019, the National Museum Cardiff held an exhibition entitled 'Tim Peake's Spacecraft'. On display was the Soyuz TMA-19M space capsule that brought British astronaut Major Tim Peake, along with crewmates Yuri Malenchenko and Tim Kopra, back to Earth after their stay on the International Space Station. An exhibition board quoted Peake after landing: 'I'm just truly elated, just the smells of Earth are so strong, it's wonderful to be back'. The poem is also informed by the exhibition's film footage of the astronauts being lifted out of the capsule.

'When I was at my most fortunate'

This poem came to life during a workshop on Japanese poetry run by Katrina Naomi. It is modelled on 'When I Was At My Most Beautiful' by Noriko Ibaragi.

'Vexiphobia'

In December 2012, Belfast City Council voted to change the policy of when to fly the Union flag at City Hall, moving to a system of designated days rather than the flag flying all year round. Within minutes of the vote, violence erupted outside which continued well into the new year. See the BBC News article 'Violence in Belfast after council votes to change Union flag policy' published online 3rd December 2012.

Acknowledgements

Thanks are due to the editors of the following publications where some of these poems first appeared: *Aberystwyth EGO, And Other Poems, Atrium, Butcher's Dog, Cheval* (2016), *Ink, Sweat & Tears, The Lampeter Review, The Lighthouse, The Lonely Crowd, Magma, The North, New Welsh Review, Planet, Poems from Snowdonia* (Seren, 2019), *Poetry Wales, The Shellshock blog.*

'Please don't take me away from Morrisons' was commended in *The Interpreter's House* Poetry Competition in 2015 and subsequently appeared in the magazine.

'Talk of her' was shortlisted in the 2016 Cornwall Contemporary Poetry Festival Competition, and subsequently appeared in *Cornish Shorts*, ed. by Emma Timpany and Felicty Notley (The History Press, 2018).

'The suitcases' was shortlisted in the 2016 *Bare Fiction* Poetry Competition.

'Three beers in, Sunset Beach, Vancouver' was commended in the 2019 Poetry Prize, Newcastle Centre for Literary Arts.

I'm grateful to Bloodaxe Books for permission to quote from Brendan Kennelly's poem 'noble', which appears in *Guff* (Bloodaxe Books, 2013).

Thanks to Leah Fritz for permission to use her comment from *The Guardian* online, and to Tamar Yoseloff who put us in touch.

A Literature Wales writers' bursary supported the early stages of writing this collection, for which I'm hugely grateful.

Thanks to all at Seren: Amy, Simon, Mick, Jamie and Sarah. You're amazing!

Thanks to those who have read these poems and given their expertise to shape them into better versions of themselves: Tiffany Atkinson, Peter Barry, Kittie Belltree, Katy Birch, Mark Blayney, Emily Blewitt, Zillah Bowes, Alice Entwistle, Creina Francis, Matthew Francis, Patrick Kavanagh, Amy McCauley, Kate North, clare e potter, Christina Thatcher, Hilary Watson, Susie Wildsmith. Huge thanks also to Gwenno Uhi for brilliant last minute checking.

And thanks to Dave, always, for everything.